How To Heal In One Day

by

MARGARITË CAMAJ

Cover by

JOSEFINA J. LUGO

I needed to heal so I wrote this in one day.
I'm sharing this with you because maybe you can heal too.

This isn't easy.
You need to believe that you are strong enough before you start.
You need to believe in yourself as much as I believe in you.

What you do in the moments of darkness ultimately defines everything. It shapes your future. It shapes your tomorrows. Every single decision—no matter how small, adds up to the outcome. What you do in the moments of darkness defines what happens to your light. Will you save it or will you let it die? It is entirely up to you.

I woke up—now what?

What do you do when you wake up feeling like this?
Feeling how, you ask? I can't explain it. It isn't something that
words can easily explain. Still, you feel it—stronger than ever.
It takes over you, almost completely.

Reread the previous page. The keyword is almost. Keep that with you. It didn't take over you completely yet. I won't let it. Neither should you.

So, now that you're up, you feel like you can't get through the day. It feels like it is impossible to get through these next 24 hours. You start to question how you will survive. I know what that feels like. Everything begins to feel a little too dark to handle. It doesn't feel like you can see light anywhere. I know. I've been there. I get you. I understand. You're not alone even though you feel like you are.

You get up and you want to talk to someone who understands. You wish that there is someone out there who gets it. You want to talk to someone who will tell you what to do so that you can feel better. You begin to search for answers. You look anywhere and everywhere for clues.

If you want to heal, you need to stop what you're doing. You're looking in the wrong places. You're not going to find the answers in the external—at least not for now.

You will not find the answers in what you are searching for. Everything that you are looking for will only give you distractions. If you want to heal, you need to redirect your search. If you want to heal, you have to try another method. You need to look for something that won't distract you. You need to find the answers to the questions that you have. You need to get to the root of the problem. You don't need to hide the problem by creating illusions.

You begin to ask yourself—what are you going to do now?

You are going to eliminate the distractions right away. Then, you are going to figure out something that not everybody figures out right away. You are going to look for the answers from no one and nothing else but yourself.

You need to look internally before you begin to look externally. You have all of the answers that you need. Many people forget that they are powerful. You can't forget. You start to think that others hold the answers and that is where you begin to forget that in order to heal, you need to focus on healing. You have to find the roots so that you can build the proper foundation.

Before we go into how you are going to heal, you need to remember to speak to yourself throughout this process. You are going to be your own best friend in the next 24 hours. Don't forget to speak to yourself with love. I've come to learn that love heals. Your mind needs to be gentle with your heart, soul, and itself. Sometimes, your mind can be a little too rough to you. We need to remind it to be more calm. Take a deep breath and repeat this reminder to yourself:

You are stronger than you believe you are. Don't forget that. You will heal.

What do you need to heal from?

First, you need to ask yourself this question: What is bothering you? What is causing you to feel like this? Do you know the reason why you woke up feeling this way? Is there one specific reason that has caused you to feel like this? Are there many reasons that have caused you to feel like this? No one knows better than you do. Dig deep within yourself.

Perhaps, there isn't something specific that you can point to. And, that is okay too. Don't be too hard on yourself. Maybe there are too many things that are going on in your life right now and you don't know how to deal with everything coming together at once. Maybe you feel like you need to heal, but you don't know the direct cause. Maybe you can't figure the problem out. Maybe there are underlying issues that cause you to feel like this. All of this is okay. Allow yourself to feel however it is that you are feeling. You can't deny yourself of your own truth.

Sit and talk to yourself for a while. I know that a lot of people think that this is abnormal, but talking to yourself is something that needs to be done. You have to know yourself. You have to learn about yourself. You have to figure out how it is that you are feeling. It is important to take the time to do that. Try to figure out the root of the problem. Sit in silence. For some, silence is scary. For you, it won't be. You will learn to be comfortable in silence. Although it may hurt, silence usually holds the truth and in the long-term, the truth will give you what is needed in order for you to survive. Inside of the silence is where you will find all of the answers. Anything else is a distraction. That is why it may feel scary at first. You are going to need to fight every single one of your fears.

Communication with others is important. But, they forget to tell you how important communication with yourself is too.

Remind yourself again:

Don't forget to be kind to your own mind while you're going through this process. You may find some things that will be painful to overcome. But, you need to go through every single emotion in order to heal. You can't ignore it. You just can't. So, don't. Go through it.

I don't want you to run away from your problems. You've made it this far. I don't want you to get scared to write down what you're going through. I want you to gain the strength and do it. Try your best. That is all that you can ask of yourself. Give it your all. You'll be surprised at how strong you are when the whole time you thought that you were weak. You'll keep discovering your power.

In the next few pages, write down some notes about what you are feeling and what is bothering you after you've spent some time reflecting.

Notes

Notes

Notes

Notes

Notes

Notes

See! You overcame your fear. Be proud of what you just did. Too many people are afraid of their own emotions. Too many people don't give themselves the chance to do what you just did. Too many people doubt their courage. That is why it takes them longer to heal. You're already on your way.

Maybe your problems are too difficult to figure out. Maybe you can't figure them out right now. Maybe you have no choice but to let it all go. Maybe it takes time. Whatever the case is, you have already begun healing—whether you are aware of it or not. You aren't going to wait for tomorrow. You are going to start today.

Now that you wrote down everything that you could think of, go back and reread everything and try to make sense of it. It might teach you a few things that you didn't know about yourself. The learning process is what will be important.

I hope you learned something new about yourself and your feelings—just like I did.

Don't be afraid if you feel like what you wrote is too much to take in. It already lived inside of you. The only difference is that you acknowledged it and you wrote it down. You took initiative to heal yourself. Don't be afraid if you feel like you still didn't solve anything. You did. You might not have solved everything. But, at least you might know the causes and how you feel. And, if you don't know the exact causes, then you at least know how you are feeling. It is not necessary to know exactly why.

That was a step in the right direction towards healing. Anything is a step as long as you don't give up. Anything is a step as long as you are diving into the problem and not ignoring it. You don't heal by ignoring. You heal by addressing it. And, we are going to continue to address it.

Remember when I said that you have the power to heal?
Remember when I said that you hold all of the answers?
Remember when I told you not to look for distractions, but,
instead, to look for the answers? I hope you remember all of
this. You're going to need this information to go on to the next
step.

I want you to think about the things that occurred in order for you to be in the situation that you are in right now. Could you have avoided something? Did you make any mistakes that led you to be in the position that you are in right now? Think.

If you made any mistakes that led you to this position, then I want you to think about them. I want you to be honest with yourself and I want you to allow this exercise to reveal all of your mistakes to you. You are human so I need you to remember that making mistakes is natural. It is absolutely normal. Don't punish yourself. Instead, reward yourself with lessons.

Don't forget that time is limited and that you need to use it wisely. Do not use this time to blame yourself for the mistakes that you have made. That will be completely pointless. You have already made those mistakes. You can't go back in time and change those errors. However, you can learn from them.

Use this time to realize your mistakes so that you could make better decisions the next time around. These mistakes may reveal some aspects of yourself that you didn't know were negatively affecting you in your decision making process. I want you to think about the mistakes in depth so that you won't end up in this position next time. These mistakes should help you see where you went wrong and what you can do to prevent any of this from occurring again—to the best of your ability. Remember that not everything is in your hands. Sometimes, the universe knows what is best for you even though you are thinking that it is rejecting you. It is possible that it is showing you a tougher journey that leads to a better outcome.

Remind yourself once again. You are not your mistakes. You are human. You have to make mistakes in order to survive—in order to learn and to better yourself. You have to make mistakes in order to reach your highest self. No one does anything perfectly. Everyone ends up in the darkness at one point or another. Sometimes it is your fault. Sometimes it is not your fault. However, it is up to you to search and to find pieces of light as quickly as you can—and heal.

Write down your mistakes. It might be intimidating to have them written down and facing you. It might be difficult to see them and to remember them. But, this is a part of the healing process. They already occurred. There is nothing to fear now. However, there is a lot to learn. Once you write them down, you will be facing your biggest teacher. Ready? Go.

Notes

Notes

Notes

Notes

Notes

Notes

Take a deep breath. You just let it all out. Forgive yourself for your mistakes. Now, you are going to use what you wrote, study it, and apply it.

Take some time and go back and reread all of your mistakes. Study your mistakes. Think about why you made them. Think about what you could have done differently in order to prevent them from occurring. Think about what you will do differently if another situation presents itself.

Whatever you do—do not start to regret what occurred. Experience was a great teacher. The mistakes were needed in order to teach you something. Everything was needed to occur for you to be where you are today. The universe has a greater purpose. You just have to push through.

Even if it seems dark, you need to keep searching for the light in the darkness. You can't pretend that the darkness is light. Remember that the darkness is where the healing takes place. However, you can't create an illusion of light. You need to find the light. There is a difference.

I know that this process can be a bit emotionally draining. That being said, I also know that everyone handles emotions differently. If you need to take a break, feel free to take a little while to just relax—in whatever way it is that you relax. Maybe you want to listen to a few songs. Maybe you want to go for a run. Maybe you want to watch a show that you enjoy. Maybe you want to cook. Do something to free your mind for a bit and then come back to this and continue it.

Think about how you felt a year ago. Think about where you were in life. Did you think that you could overcome a few hard times to get to where you are today?

Think about the things that you have overcome that you didn't think that you could get through. Think about the times when you felt like everything was dark. Eventually, you found some light, right? Eventually, you found that there was a reason that all of this occurred, right? There is hope. Remind yourself of that. It is necessary.

Close your eyes. I want you to think about this past year. I want you to think about some of the hard times that you went through. You didn't think that you could have gotten through them, right?

Now, I want you to write down a few things that you overcame within the past year that you didn't think that you could get through. I want you to do this so that you can remind yourself that some things happen for a reason, but that you have a huge impact on what the outcome will be. This will be shaped by how you act in your darkest moments.

Notes

Notes

Notes

Notes

Notes

Go back and reread everything that you just wrote one time.
Pay attention to what you find.

Every single thing that you did took strength. You might not have thought that you could have gotten through it, but you did nevertheless. Think about this when you think about the current position that you are in. You can get through this, too. Sometimes, you need to remind yourself of the past in order to understand your present and shape your future.

Now, I want you to think about how you want to feel tomorrow. How do you want to wake up feeling? What would be ideal for tomorrow? For some of you, thinking about tomorrow might be difficult because you don't know how you will get through today. If you have faith, you will. Write down everything that you would want to feel tomorrow in the next few pages.

Notes

Notes

Notes

Notes

Notes

Notes

Everything that you just wrote is what already existed in the thoughts inside of your mind. That means that if your mind could have thought it, you are capable of feeling it. Don't automatically dismiss it. Maybe you can't heal every single thing right away, but you are definitely walking towards it.

Now, I want you to think about where you will be in a year from now. I want you to think about your problems and which one of your problems will actually be relevant in a year from now. I want you to think about which problems won't be relevant at all.

Use this as a tool to help you figure out what is important and what is not. This realization will help you possibly heal even faster. You won't be wasting time trying to fix what you have no power over or what won't matter in a year from today. Work on fixing what will matter.

In the next couple of pages, write down where you want to be in a year from now. Most importantly, write down how you want to feel in a year from now. Don't forget to filter out what is relevant and what isn't relevant.

Notes

Notes

Notes

Notes

Notes

Notes

Go back and reread what you wrote once again—just like you have reread everything else that you have previously written. It is always good to go back and to try to understand what you feel after you write it down. You will always see it from a different perspective.

I bet that you don't want to feel how you are feeling today. I bet that you want to feel happy. I bet that you do not want to feel like you are in the darkness all the time and that there is no escape. I bet that you want to be filled with light.

I bet that you want to be healed.

So, now that you are not distracted, but fully immersed—try to connect how you were feeling when you first started reading this and compare it to how you are feeling now. Has anything changed? Has anything improved? Do you feel a little better?

I want you to think about everything that is currently on your mind. I want you to think about how you feel at the moment. I want you to think about what you are feeling right now and try to analyze it.

You are going to go deep into your emotions on the next few pages one more time. Take some time to sit with your feelings. Try to feel them all out at this moment. Do not think about how you were feeling earlier. When you are done feeling out your emotions, start to write.

Notes

Notes

Notes

Notes

Notes

Notes

As you have been doing for these exercises, go back and reread everything that you have written. Try to understand what you are currently feeling. Has anything changed? Has your perspective regarding today changed at all? Are you better than when you first woke up? Did you gain more understanding? These are things to think about.

Now, go back to the first writing exercise and see how you felt when you first started reading this book. Try to compare how you felt and how you are currently feeling. Are there any differences? Look deeper and try to figure them out.

If you feel like some parts of you are still completely in the darkness and did not improve at all, I want you to write them down on the next page.

Notes

Ask yourself, is this fixable? If so, what can you do to improve it? Is there anything that you can do to fix it right now? If there is, write what you can do to fix the problem on the next page.

Notes

Work on fixing what you can. Start now. If it is not possible to begin to fix it today, then start tomorrow. Start whenever you can. Just remember, do not avoid beginning to fix the problem by distracting yourself. Focus on what will help you heal.

If there is nothing that you can do to fix the problem, then you must continue to feel out the emotions and try to get through it to the best of your ability. Practice healing. Allow yourself to feel everything possible, even if it is all negative. As much as it hurts, you need to allow yourself to feel in order to heal.

Write down a few things that make you happy on the next page.

Notes

Write down a few good character traits that you have on the next page.

Notes

Write down what brings you peace on the next page.

Notes

Write down what you are currently grateful for on the next page.

Notes

Remember that you are filled with light. No matter what you feel at the moment. You can get through anything if you allow yourself to go through it. Your mind is an extremely powerful tool. You just have to let it help you instead of harm you. You have the power to save yourself. Love yourself enough to do that. You are counting on you. Little you is counting on you. When the world seems too tough, hold on. You will heal. You are worthy of healing. I promise.

I know that you feel like you are by yourself.
I know that you think that you can't do it alone.
But, you can.
You can wipe those tears all by yourself.
You know what you know even when no one else does.
Even though there are moments when you don't think you do.
You do,
especially if you search deep enough—
especially if you look long-term instead of short-term.
When you feel like you are stuck in the dirt and no one will
reach out a hand to help you,
I hope that you throw seeds all over the floor and get yourself
out.
The universe will help you by bringing you water.
Experience will help you grow.
You will teach yourself to grow—
through your mistakes,
through the dark times.
Use those tears to grow
into a flower.

You are now familiar with what you can do.

You are now familiar with the strength that you have.

You are now familiar with the power that you have inside of you.

You have to heal yourself.
And, you can.
I prayed for you.

;